TABLE OF CONTENTS

CHAPTER 1

BUILDING FOR THE FUTURE

Imagine you are taking a ride through your state's capital on a field trip. You pass a statue of an important person in history. Raising your phone to the window, you snap a photo. Your friend couldn't go on the trip. So you send her the picture along with a couple of silly smiley faces to let her know what's happening. You arrive at the big, fancy capitol building with your classmates. It towers over you as you crane your neck to look up. At your teacher's instruction, you take out your notebook and pen to jot down notes about important government positions during the tour. You learn about the taxes the government collects and how that money is used to help people.

From monuments and huge buildings, such as that statue and your state capitol, to everyday things, you can find origins deep in the past. Even such things as writing

Like grand buildings of today, the Egyptian monuments were built to impress. The main temple at Abu Simbel features four huge statues, each 66 feet (20 meters) tall, of the king that built it—Ramses II (reigned 1279–1213 BC).

with pen and paper for school assignments or texting friends with emojis aren't exactly new. The modern world is full of ideas and inventions that date back thousands of years to the civilization of ancient Egypt. Large building projects, taxes, and even predicting the weather have roots in this civilization, which came to an end more than 2,000 years ago.

The people of ancient Egypt lived in North Africa and built their civilization along the Nile River.

WHO WERE THE ANCIENT EGYPTIANS, ANYWAY?

The civilization of ancient Egypt started more than 5,000 years ago and lasted for around 3,000 years. It was not only one of the first civilizations but one of the longest lasting. The Egyptians built a complex society with well-organized farming. At the same time, humans in many other parts of the world were living as isolated groups. They survived by hunting animals and gathering plants to eat. The ancient Egyptians were more than just farmers. They also built huge, amazing wonders such as the famous pyramids and the sphinx because of their beliefs. The Egyptians were often inspired by the many gods of their religion. This religion was central to Egyptian life, and the people believed the pharaoh, their ruler, was a living god. Their structures, built for gods, survived to amaze later civilizations even after Egypt was conquered in 332 BC and later invaded.

BUILDING PYRAMIDS

Walk around a modern city and you'll find yourself looking up to see huge projects going on around you. Cranes lift giant metal girders and stone blocks into place on towering office and apartment buildings, shopping malls, and much more. Teams of construction workers operate the machinery and swarm all over the buildings. These vast projects can seem as if they could only happen in the modern world. However, the ancient Egyptians were not strangers to major building projects that employed a huge workforce. Modern architects and builders are still learning from their work.

Made of painted wood figurines, a tomb model of bakers from the time of the Middle Kingdom offers a clear glimpse into ancient Egyptian daily life. Such models were believed to provide benefits in the afterlife, such as increased wealth.

In fact, even modern engineers have not been able to improve on some of the amazing inventions of ancient Egypt. Because the Egyptians had little contact with the other societies that existed at the same time, they had to invent ways to create everything they used. These discoveries included skills such as metalworking and glassblowing. Many of their techniques in these areas are still used today. Plus, the great pyramids they constructed have stood for around 4,500 years. Building giant, lasting structures like those takes a lot of knowledge!

EGYPT'S INFLUENCE

Ancient Egyptian art and other beautiful objects can still be seen in museums around the world. The Egyptians buried these priceless treasures in tombs because they believed that dead people could use them in the afterlife. Even the bodies of the dead were mummified to preserve them. This helps us to understand more about how the Egyptians lived. It also helps us see how much of our modern world is based on ideas and innovations that started on the banks of the Nile River more than 5,000 years ago. Throughout history, other societies have been inspired by and have learned from the ancient Egyptians. One of the main reasons for this lasting influence is because people today know much more about the Egyptians than other ancient civilizations that existed at the same time. Egypt's hot, dry climate is especially good for preserving objects for thousands of years. Modern scholars have been able to decipher the Egyptians' system of writing. The Egyptians also believed in creating things that would last a long time.

Ask anyone what they know about ancient Egypt and they'll probably mention the pyramids at Giza. They are some of the most famous, amazing landmarks in the world. The Great Pyramid of Khufu, the largest of the pyramids, has a square base measuring about 755 feet (230 meters) on each side. The length of each side and the angles needed to make an exact pyramid shape are almost perfect. The pyramid is made of 2,300,000 stone blocks, weighing 2.6 tons (2.4 tonnes) each. These blocks had to be moved into their precise positions without cranes or even wheeled vehicles. The Great Pyramid was the world's tallest structure for more than 3,800 years.

So what impact have these famous structures had on modern building? First of all, the pyramids were among the first major buildings in the world built from stone. Stone is strong enough to build large and long-

The Great Pyramid of Khufu was built about 2500 BC. Khufu was a king of Egypt in the fourth dynasty.

lasting structures. It seems obvious to us to think of stone blocks as the building material for large buildings. But the Egyptians had no steel tools to cut and shape the stones. Cutting each block would have been a huge job for a team of workers.

STATUS SYMBOLS

Remember that imaginary trip to your state's capitol building? Many of our largest buildings are built to impress people. Huge government and office buildings show the wealth and power of the people and corporations who build them. The Capitol Building in Washington, D.C., illustrates the power of the U.S. government. The ancient Egyptians created giant buildings to show off their power, and the pyramids are the most awesome examples of this. Each one was built as the tomb of an Egyptian king, or pharaoh. They are much bigger than they need to be as they are solid structures with only small burial chambers and passages inside. These monuments would remind Egyptians of the power of the kings buried inside.

SECURITY

When you own something worth a lot of money, where do you put it to keep it safe? You might hide it in your home or use a safety deposit box at a bank. Or perhaps you just remember to lock your doors! Still, homes with valuables or buildings such as banks are targets for

The pyramids have extra passages and chambers, and experts are still uncertain of the uses of all of them. Some may have been used to confuse tomb robbers. A few passages are dead ends. One clear security measure in the Great Pyramid was a series of granite slabs that slid down in tracks to block the entrance of the King's Chamber.

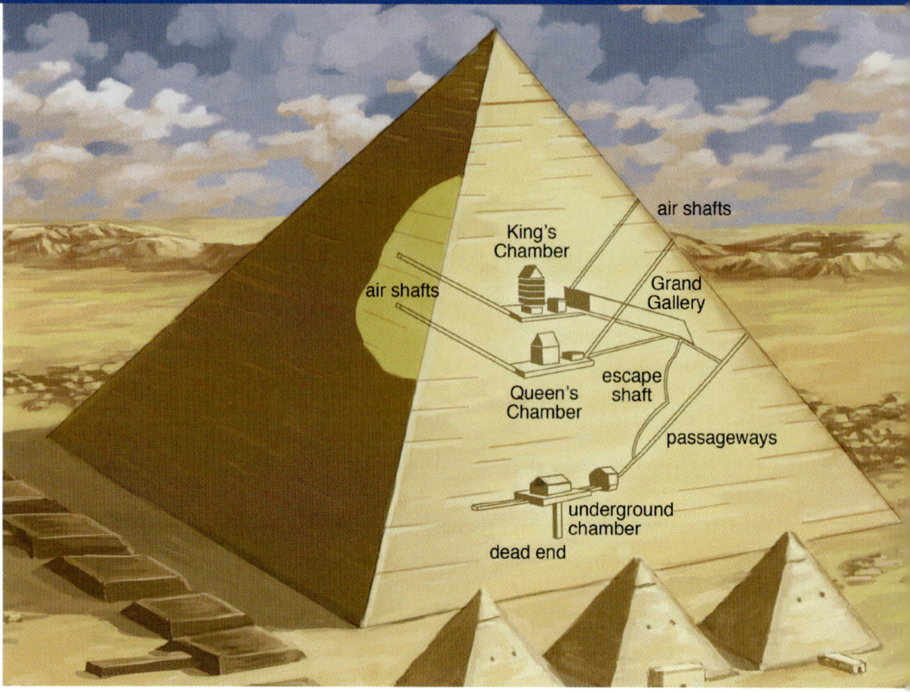

robbers. Even with locks, the most important modern buildings also have other security features such as alarms and cameras to deter criminals. Likewise, the pyramids were targets for robbers desperate to get their hands on the riches buried with the pharaohs. These tombs also included some of the world's first security measures. Such measures included curses carved on the walls to turn thieves away and tunnels filled with rubble to keep them out. Even so, many pyramids were robbed soon after the tombs were sealed.

PERIODS OF EGYPT

Ancient Egypt went through several changes over its 3,000 years. Its history is divided into the following periods.

3100 BC:

Upper and Lower Egypt united under one king

2686–2181 BC:

Old Kingdom; building of the pyramids at Giza

2025–1700 BC:

Middle Kingdom

1550–1069 BC:

New Kingdom; pharaohs such as Tutankhamun and Ramses II buried in the Valley of the Kings

332 BC:

Egypt taken over by Macedonian king Alexander the Great

30 BC:

Roman invasion of Egypt and death of the last queen of Egypt, Cleopatra VII

Periods between the Old, Middle, and New Kingdoms were times of unrest with different groups and kings battling for control.

FACT

We even know the name of the person who came up with the pyramid. Imhotep was the chief adviser of the pharaoh Djoser. He devised the shape of the step pyramid that became Djoser's tomb. It was built around 2650 BC.

When banks want to keep money or valuables secure, they store them underground in a vault with solid walls and bombproof doors. By Egypt's New Kingdom period, kings decided that pyramids were too obvious a target for criminals. They started to build underground tombs dug into the rocky sides of an area called the Valley of the Kings. Hiding the tombs behind secret doorways, they hoped to stay one step ahead of the tomb robbers.

TOMB DECORATORS

Do you think you could be a professional interior designer for a home? What about a professional designer for a tomb! The ancient Egyptian underground tombs were decked out using many of the skills that are still in use today, from plastering to painting. Plasterers added a smooth surface to the rock, which designers and painters then covered with scenes from life in ancient Egypt. Carpenters and stonemasons also worked to ensure the tombs were suitable for a king or queen.

Modern construction workers may use different tools, but their jobs are not so different from Egyptian builders. However, there were many more people at work on an Egyptian construction site than today's typical building sites. Up to 100,000 workers took about 20 years to build a pyramid. Many of these pyramid builders only worked for part of the year. They worked while the Nile River was in flood before returning to farm their land. While working on the pyramid, some of them were given housing in specially built villages, along with good food and even medical care.

Egypt is not the only place where you will find pyramids. Other ancient civilizations, such as the Maya of the Americas, built pyramids of their own. These step pyramids did not have the smooth sides of the Egyptian tombs. The shape of the pyramids is often used in modern buildings. Sometimes the whole building is a pyramid, but more often pyramid shapes are added to roofs and other features of buildings.

This pyramid at the Louvre Museum in Paris, France, is one of the most famous modern examples.

BUILDING FOR THE GODS

Since the end of ancient Egyptian civilization, temples, churches, and mosques have been built for worshippers of many different religions, such as Judaism, Christianity, and Islam. Some of the most impressive Egyptian buildings were also temples, built to worship the many Egyptian gods. As with pyramids, these temples were usually built of stone, so they have survived to inspire later builders. Temples included large halls, with roofs supported by giant columns, statues, and carvings around the walls. All these features have influenced modern builders of places of worship and other public buildings.

OBELISKS

If you visit the Washington Monument in our nation's capitol, you'll be looking at a shape directly inspired by ancient Egypt—the obelisk. In New York City's Central Park and beside the River Thames in London, you can see real Egyptian obelisks. These solid stone monuments were built to last.

Obelisks have a square base and four sides, which the Egyptians covered with carvings. The top is shaped like a pyramid. They usually stood alongside the entrances to temples. An engraving on one obelisk from around 1450 BC reveals that it took seven months to carve this single block of stone out of a quarry.

The granite obelisk in New York City's Central Park, known as Cleopatra's Needle, was originally located in Egypt. Egypt gave it to the U.S. in the late 1800s as an exchange for funds. The giant structure was shipped over the ocean and placed in Central Park in 1881.

BUILDING FOR THE PEOPLE

Today, we have street addresses to identify where we live. We can usually use city blocks to figure out how to get around. Like many modern cities, Egyptian towns were built on a grid system. Streets crisscrossed each other and individual houses joined together in terraces. Ancient Egyptians had their names written on their front doors so the officials knew who lived there.

However, modern houses and ancient alike were not generally built from huge blocks of stone like the pyramids and temples. Instead they were built from materials such as wood and brick. Ancient Egyptian houses were constructed from mud bricks, as humans had used even long before them. Brickmakers mixed

The village of Deir el-Medina on the west bank of the Nile River housed the tomb workers, including craftsmen and builders. The foundations survive in ruins and can be visited today.

river mud, water, and usually straw in a mold and left the bricks to dry in the sun. Bricks are still made like this in some parts of the world. Wood was in short supply in the deserts of Egypt, so it was not usually used as a building material, except for supports and door frames. Workers' houses may only have had a few rooms, with a flat roof for sleeping on in the hot Egyptian climate.

You'd probably be more comfortable in the houses of the rich. Modern houses are built with separate bedrooms for sleeping. Only the wealthier Egyptian families enjoyed separate bedrooms and shower rooms. However, showers

FACT

Wherever food is stored, pests such as rats and mice will try to eat it. The ancient Egyptians invented a rat trap to deal with this problem. It was a box that allowed the animal to enter but then slid shut to prevent it from escaping.

were very basic. They involved a servant pouring water over a master's or mistress's head.

We can even thank the ancient Egyptians for inventing something like the modern toilet. One house belonging to a scribe named Nakht contains one of the oldest toilets discovered. It was a seat with a hole in it and a bucket of sand underneath.

LIGHTING THE WAY

How often do you travel by boat? Even if it's not very often, day and night, ships are constantly crossing the oceans carrying goods and people around the world. In the dark or in bad weather, the crews of these ships rely on lights and lighthouses along with electronic navigation aids. These aids warn them of dangers along the coast, such as rocks or areas of shallow water. These lighthouses are all inspired by one of the most famous buildings in ancient Egypt—the great lighthouse, or Pharos of Alexandria.

This towering structure stood on an island at the harbor entrance of Alexandria. It may have been about 350 feet (107 m) tall and lit by a huge fire at the top to guide ships into the harbor.

Just as in any modern city, Egyptian building techniques changed and new ideas developed over the centuries. The Pharos was built in about 280 BC under Greek influence, near the end of Egyptian civilization.

CHAPTER 2

RIVER OF LIFE

Most of us buy our food packaged from supermarkets or sometimes fast-food restaurants when we're in a hurry. It's easy to forget that almost everything we eat starts its life on a farm. Modern farms use the latest technologies to help grow our food. But many of the basic techniques of farming have not changed since the earliest civilizations. And the ancient Egyptians helped to develop a lot of these techniques.

All crops need water to grow and all animals need water to stay alive. There was very little rain in ancient Egypt. Most water had to come from the Nile River. The area of fertile land next to the river was called the Black Land. The barren desert beyond was the Red Land. Egypt's people lived and farmed on the Black Land.

A felucca boat is a wooden craft with an open deck designed for shallow water. The basic design of modern felucca boats remains the same as in ancient Egypt.

RIVER TRANSPORT

The easiest way to get around ancient Egypt was the Nile River. The river was home to everything from small fishing boats to large barges carrying the blocks of rock used in Egyptian buildings. For the Egyptians, a poor man was someone who had no boat. Egyptian boats were made from reeds and later wood. Some of the most important features of sailing boats were invented in ancient Egypt. These included sails that could be angled to allow a boat to sail into the wind and a rudder for steering. Some boats on the Nile have changed little since ancient times.

Just as today's farmers might wish for a rainy season to water their fields, the Egyptians awaited the Nile flood every year. Between July and October the fields along the river would flood. The farmers could only watch and worry. If the floodwaters got too high, the land would be ruined. If they remained too low, crops would not grow and people would starve.

WATERING THE CROPS

Do you live in an area where the weather changes all the time? You might check the forecast on an app to figure out what to wear to school. Will it be rainy or chilly? Thanks to the weather forecasters who use complex computer programs and data about weather patterns, you can plan ahead. The ancient Egyptians also understood the importance of forecasting the weather, and particularly the Nile flood. They built steps called "nilometers" along the riverbanks. These steps into the river were used to measure how high the water rose so flood levels could be predicted more accurately.

Today, many farmers can use sprinklers and other equipment to irrigate, or water, their fields. The Egyptians developed a large-scale irrigation system. At the time of the flood, the people created a system of linked embankments, ditches, and canals. This organized system spread the floodwater over an area as wide as possible. The project of irrigating the fields during the flood involved a huge amount of organization and was led by skilled engineers.

Ancient Egypt's farmers invented a device called a shaduf to lift water from the river. This tool used a weight at one end of a pole to enable farmers to lift much more water than they ever could with a bucket. Farmers used the shaduf for many centuries after the end of ancient Egypt until electric pumps eventually replaced it. However, the shaduf is so simple and effective that some rural Egyptians still use it today.

The ancient shaduf design can still be seen in use today. It works like a seesaw with a rope to lower a bucket on one end and a weight on the other.

IN THE FIELDS

Today's farmers use massive mechanical tools such as tractors and harvesters to plow and harvest their fields. Egyptian farmers may not have had wheeled vehicles, but they invented tools that are still used today. Plows were used to turn over the soil in the fields before planting the year's crops. Instead of tractors, these plows were pulled by cattle.

Gardeners today would be familiar with some of the tools used by Egyptian farmers, including hoes and pitchforks. Curved sickles were used to harvest crops. However, the Egyptians were not able to make iron blades. Most of these tools had blades made from sharpened wood and softer metals such as copper.

A small tomb model shows an ancient Egyptian plow. Real Egyptian plows were made of wood and dug up rows for planting seeds for crops.

WHAT DID THE ANCIENT EGYPTIANS EAT?

You would recognize most of the things the ancient Egyptians ate. Today, the main crops grown in many parts of the world are grains such as wheat and barley. Wheat is mainly used to make bread. The Egyptians were some of the first people to grow these crops in a large-scale and organized way. Plus, their wheat was also baked into bread. Ancient Egyptian farmers grew a wide range of vegetables, which needed much more water than the fields of wheat. Most people did not eat much meat, because they had no way of refrigeration to keep meat fresh. However, the rich would eat meats such as beef and lamb. Fish from the Nile River was another great source of food.

CHAPTER 3

GETTING ORGANIZED

Imagine what life would be like if there was no government to make decisions that affect you and your community. What if there was no one to organize schools or the building of roads. In democratic countries we vote for local representatives and others to lead. They make decisions for the whole city or country, deciding what to do about things like education and healthcare that affect all of us. If we don't like the decisions they make, we can vote for different leaders. The leaders we choose are supported by experienced officials.

The ancient Egyptians did not have the chance to vote for their leaders. The pharaoh was the political and religious leader of ancient Egypt. Pharaohs normally inherited power from their father or another family member. Even so, in times of rebellion, Egypt's ruling classes violently tried to seize power from each other. However, many of the other ways we choose to organize and govern societies are similar to those of the ancient Egyptians.

EGYPT UNITED

If you have a backyard, you probably know where it ends so you don't get in trouble with a neighbor. Today, we like to know where our property begins and ends. The whole world is divided into nations or countries. But most ancient civilizations did not have clear borders. In other civilizations, rulers would often control a city and the land around it. In contrast, the ancient Egyptians had clear ideas about where their land started and ended. The pharaoh controlled all of Egypt from the cataract, or rapids, of the Nile near Aswan in the south to the sea in the north. The country was made up of Upper Egypt in the south and Lower Egypt in the north. A true pharaoh of ancient Egypt had to control both halves, and for most of its history, Egypt's borders changed little. During the New Kingdom period, Egypt's armies invaded neighboring lands to create an Egyptian empire.

Today, we also like to know who's in charge of what. There were levels of government and organization in Egypt, just like in a modern country. Countries are often divided into areas such as states and counties, each with its own officials. For most of Egyptian history, there were

Upper and Lower Egypt were first united in about 3100 BC by King Narmer. This event is shown on a carving called the Narmer Palette.

42 nomes. Nomes were divisions of land. Each nome had a local governor, called a nomarch, who reported to the pharaoh and central government. Records show that the things they reported on were similar to what modern officials might keep track of. Examples include how much they collected in taxes, crime figures, and what they spent.

We all pay taxes to our government. A chunk of the money people earn from their jobs or what we spend shopping goes to the government. This money pays for the services that everyone needs. Ancient Egypt was one of the first societies to develop a tax system that applied to everyone. The Egyptians did not have money so a portion of the wheat and other crops that people grew

In the later periods, ancient Egypt was divided into 42 sections called nomes. About half of the nomes were located in Upper Egypt, where the Nile empties into the Mediterranean Sea. The other 22 nomes were divisions running along the Nile in Lower Egypt.

were handed to the government as tax. Poorer people paid their tax by working for the pharaoh. They would spend part of the year on major building projects such as pyramids and temples.

The ancient Egyptians also devised a very early form of social security to help people when times were hard and they did not have enough to eat. Taxes paid in food were stored in the pharaoh's granaries. If the Nile flood failed and the harvest was poor, food was distributed to keep the people alive.

A sculpture of a scribe at work dates back to the period of the Old Kingdom.

LIFE OF A SCRIBE

One of the main keys to running a strong government and economy is having capable and efficient people managing it. The ancient Egyptians were some of the first people to understand the importance of this idea. They had special schools to educate the government officials called scribes. When most people could not read and write, scribes were very powerful. They kept all sorts of official records including the laws of Egypt, reports, and accounts. Scribes also took senior jobs in the army and other areas of Egyptian life.

ORGANIZING WORKERS

We think that a business employing thousands of workers is a relatively new thing. Modern corporations started in the factories of the Industrial Revolution in the past 200 years. However, Egyptian officials were also experts in organizing large numbers of workers, whether to build pyramids or irrigate the fields.

Administrators had to have detailed records of the people so they could summon workers when needed. They also arranged the supplies of stone, wood, and other materials needed for a project.

Just as in a modern workforce, projects did not always run smoothly. If workers are unhappy with their bosses or how much they are paid, they may refuse to work. This is called going on strike. The first workers' strike we know of took place in about 1100 BC when royal tomb builders stopped working because they had not been paid. These valued workers had regular hours of work and days off. They were paid in grain every month.

Pharaoh Ramses II (reigned 1279-1213 BC), one of the most powerful rulers in the history of ancient Egypt, built many of Egypt's most impressive monuments. His military exercises were expensive and depended on efficient administration and tax collection.

CHAPTER 4

READING, WRITING, AND ARITHMETIC

If we know how to read and write, we can communicate with anyone anywhere who understands our language. This communication could be on paper, on screen, or even on a billboard or the side of a building. It could be in a text message to a friend or a book or website seen by thousands of people. Writing also lets us communicate across time. We still read books and other forms of writing created thousands of years ago.

As with so many things, the ancient Egyptians were among the first people to have a written language. Writing started in the Sumerian civilization around the same time. The first evidence of Egyptian writing dates from about 3250 BC. In fact, writing is central to so much of what we know about ancient Egypt. The Egyptians produced a huge quantity of writing from tax records to personal letters. Most of this writing was done by a small group of people. The average Egyptian could not read and write.

The most well-known form of ancient Egyptian writing was the painting or carving of elaborate hieroglyphs. This hieroglyphic writing used beautiful images and symbols. But you probably don't spell out every word or use proper grammar every time you text a friend. Neither did the Egyptians use the formal hieroglyphics all the time. They also used more informal ways of writing. These were called hieratic and demotic script and could be written and understood by a wider range of people.

The most well-known form of ancient Egyptian writing was the painting or carving of elaborate hieroglyphs.

English and many other modern languages use symbols to represent sounds—we call them letters. For the most part, hieroglyphs work in the same way, using pictures to represent different sounds and words with rules for use. Similar to picture writing in its earliest forms, many of us also use pictures and symbols to represent whole words or phrases. We might insert emojis into messages instead of typing out the words. We also use symbols for all kinds of communication, including road signs or the icons that appear on your computer screen.

Early hieroglyphs were mostly carved or painted on the walls of tombs and temples. Just as people create art for places of worship today, this beautiful script showed respect for the Egyptian gods. Hieratic script used similar symbols but was quicker and easier to write. It was used in official reports, letters, and many other documents.

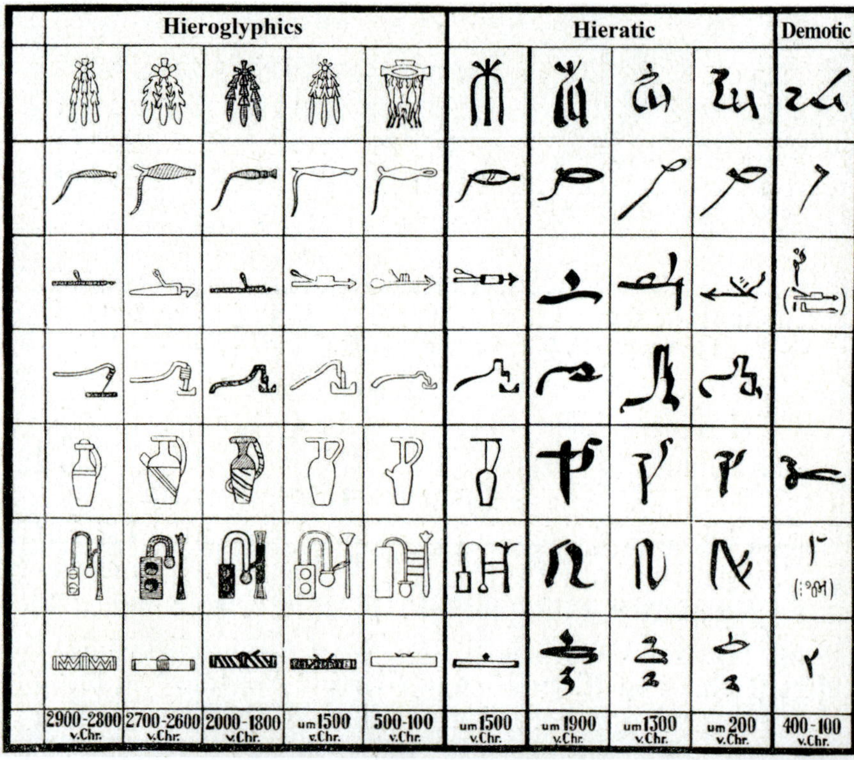

Hieroglyphics were the most elaborate symbols. The hieratic script was a simplified version often used for writing with ink on papyrus. Finally, demotic script was a form that began to replace the hieratic in about 660 BC except for in more formal documents.

The Rosetta Stone is currently on display in the British Museum in London, United Kingdom. The stone is black granite and about 3 feet (90 centimeters) tall and 2 feet (60 cm) wide.

DECODING EGYPTIAN WRITING

The Rosetta Stone is a stone slab that holds the key to our understanding of ancient Egypt. When the Egyptian civilization came to an end, understanding of Egyptian hieroglyphic writing died with it. The Rosetta Stone was discovered in 1799 in a village called Rosetta. It contains the same inscription in ancient Greek and two versions of the Egyptian language. Egypt's ruler at the time was Greek but the inscription was written to be read by Egyptian priests. When the Stone was discovered, people could read ancient Greek, so they could use it to figure out how hieroglyphs worked. After many years trying to crack the code, Frenchman Jean-Francois Champollion figured out the secrets of Egyptian hieroglyphs in 1822.

PAPYRUS

Even with the move to digital books and notes, you probably still use paper all the time. Notebooks, sticky tags, and paperback novels are still handy when your devices run out of battery power! The word *paper* has its roots in ancient Egypt. It comes from the papyrus reed, which was one of the most essential materials in ancient Egypt. Modern paper is mostly made from wood pulp, but the Egyptians used papyrus reeds to make paper.

The tall reeds that grew by the Nile were harvested and sliced into narrow strips. These strips were combined in two layers with water and beaten with stones. This

A copy of The Book of the Dead from about 1050 BC is a scroll that measures more than 17 feet long! The oldest papyrus sheets ever discovered are around 4,500 years old.

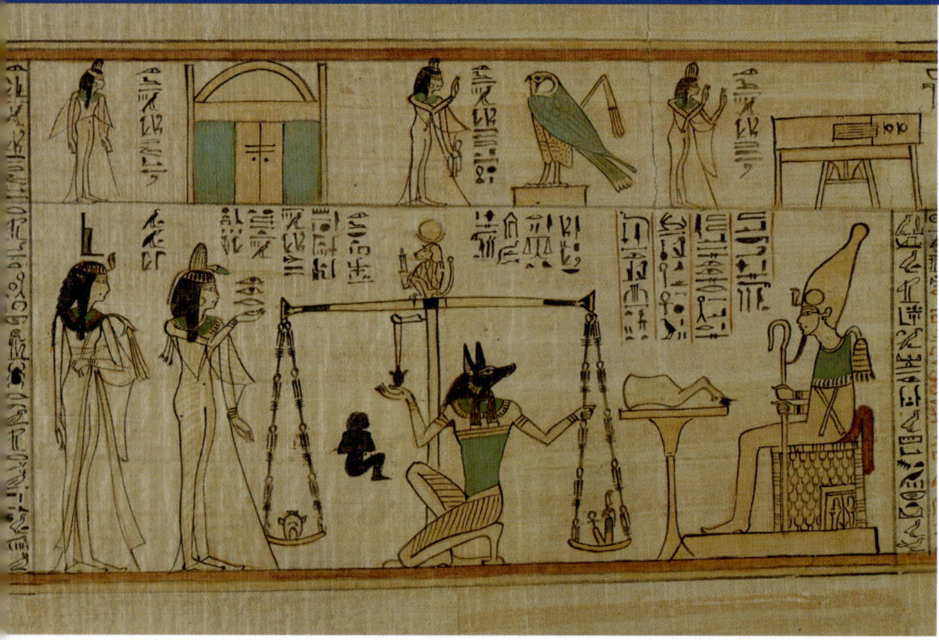

created the paper that the Egyptians used to write official reports, love poems, prayers, letters, and much more.

Single papyrus sheets were used for letters and short documents. But more often they were stuck together to make long scrolls with many pages. These first books could be up to 130 feet (40 m) long and were wound around wooden rods. Egyptian scribes were probably the first people to write with ink. Each scribe carried a special pack containing red and black ink and reed brushes for drawing characters on the papyrus.

STARTING SCHOOLS

Have you ever sat in school and wondered who came up with the idea of getting young people together for classes? You'll find part of the answer in ancient Egypt. In early societies, children could learn from their parents or others in their community. When societies such as ancient Egypt started using written language, they needed to teach young people how to read and write it. When they grew up, these young people became the pharaoh's scribes and officials.

Unlike most societies today, only the lucky few could attend school in ancient Egypt. School was for children who were expected to become government officials, scribes, or priests. Some schools also specialized in training doctors, much like modern medical colleges.

Usually, schools were for boys only, although girls from wealthy families were sometimes taught to write at home.

Some aspects of Egyptian schools have been followed by schools ever since, including focusing on reading, writing, and math. Fortunately, schools have moved on in other areas. For example, Egyptian teachers believed in tough discipline and students were often beaten. One list of rules for teachers stated that "a boy's ear is on his back," meaning that regular beatings would help students to learn.

COMIC CAPERS

What's your favorite cartoon? Or think of the latest meme. Pictures can sometimes be a lot funnier than words alone! Next time you read or watch a cartoon, remember that this mix of art and humor goes back to ancient Egypt. Egyptian jokes were often visual. These include papyri (the plural of *papyrus*) and tomb paintings showing cats chasing mice and animals performing human jobs. There are even examples of hieroglyphs being used to show speech bubbles, just like comic strips today.

MATHEMATICS AND MEASURING

Have you ever thought about why we count in 10s? When we get past 9, we add 1 in the next column and start again. We are so used to it that it's difficult to imagine any other way of counting. Like so much of what we know about math, this system started with the ancient Egyptians. Math was an essential part of a scribe's education.

The Egyptians introduced their number system based on 10s by about 2700 BC. It was probably inspired by the 10 fingers on our hands. Different symbols were used for multiples of 10, so hundreds were shown as coils of rope and thousands shown as lotus plants.

Geometry is the branch of math concerned with calculating shapes and angles. It is essential for all sorts of modern uses, including engineering and building. The Egyptians were masters of geometry and were able to calculate the area of a circle and the volume of a pyramid.

FACT

The Rhind Mathematical Papyrus gives us lots of information about Egyptian math. It was a manual for trainee administrators created in around 1550 BC. Scribes could learn everything from how to calculate the slope of a pyramid's sides to the amount of food geese would eat. The way Egyptians multiplied numbers is very similar to the process modern computers use.

MEASURING TIME AND SPACE

Today, we divide the year into 12 months with a total of 365 days. Our calendar has changed over the centuries. People have learned more about the movements of Earth and other bodies in space, such as the Earth's journey around the sun. The ancient Egyptians did not understand that Earth orbits around the sun. Yet, just as we do today, they used a yearly calendar based on 365 days, each 24 hours long. Each of 12 months had 30 days and then they added extra days to the final month. The new year started at the beginning of the Nile flood every year.

A tomb painting shows Egyptian daily life, including harvesting crops. Math was always practical for such activities of daily life. It was designed to measure things like the area of fields and the weight of crops for calculating taxes.

It was not just in measuring time that the ancient Egyptians led the way. Many of the measurements we use were originally based on parts of the body, such as the foot. An inch is supposed to be roughly the width of a human thumb. The ancient Egyptians used the same method, measuring size in cubits, which were about the length of a man's forearm. A cubit was divided into thumb-widths and palm-widths.

The Egyptian cubit influenced the measurement system of other ancient people.

CUBIT STICKS

When measuring huge construction projects, such as the pyramids, it was not enough just to use someone's forearm. The measurements were all slightly different. The Egyptians made a piece of stone that was the standard cubit. Then scribes and builders would have a wooden cubit stick measured from the official stone example. The Egyptians also had standard weights that were used in measuring the amount and value of goods such as grain.

CHAPTER 5

LOOKING GOOD AND HAVING FUN

People everywhere love to be seen in the latest fashions. But following fashion trends is nothing new. Paintings and statues of the ancient Egyptians show that the upper class of Egyptian society were fashion followers who really cared about what they looked like.

Today, the latest styles in clothes or makeup may be worn and promoted by celebrities and fashion designers. Wealthy Egyptians took their fashion leads from the pharaoh and the royal household, wanting to look good.

Over nearly 3,000 years of Egyptian civilization, fashions changed. However, the main material for Egyptian clothes was always linen, which we still wear today. Linen is made from the fibers of the flax plant. The linen tunics worn by common people were quite rough, but the wealthy could afford the finest smooth fabric.

A painting in a New Kingdom period tomb shows Egyptian fashion. The figures are painted wearing white clothing.

T-shirts and jeans are worn by both men and women today. Our regular comfortable clothes are pretty much the same for everyone. Egyptian clothes were similar for both men and women too. Most average Egyptian families wore simple linen skirts and tunics, keeping people cool and protecting them from the heat of the sun.

FACT

The world's oldest woven garment comes from ancient Egypt. The Tarkhan dress was found in an Egyptian tomb and is more than 5,000 years old. With tailored sleeves and pleats, it would have been the height of fashion when it was first worn.

FINE FOOTWEAR

When you put on a pair of sandals or flip-flops, you are following in the footsteps of the pharaoh Tutankhamun (King Tut). His tomb contained many pairs of sandals made from palm leaves, papyrus, or leather. All of these were probably more comfortable than the pharaoh's gold ceremonial sandals. We know that Tutankhamun wore socks with his sandals as several pairs were buried with him. Have you ever tried to wear socks with flip-flops? The Egyptians invented a sort-of toe sock with a separate space for the big toe!

MAKEUP AND BEAUTY

A wealthy ancient Egyptian would feel right at home browsing through the cosmetics, jewelery, and perfumes of a modern department store. Many of the things that people wear to make themselves more attractive were worn in ancient Egypt.

> Many of the things that people wear to make themselves more attractive were first worn in ancient Egypt.

Modern eye makeup has been influenced by the dark kohl Egyptian men and women wore around their eyes. This would make their eyes appear darker, but it also had a practical purpose as it reduced the glare of the dazzling desert sun.

The ancient Egyptians believed in keeping clean.

A painting of three women in the tomb of Nakht is an example of artwork that shows the dark kohl makeup Egyptians wore around their eyes.

They also believed in clean, white teeth. One papyrus includes a recipe for toothpaste made with rock salt, mint, and pepper. They also kept themselves smelling fresh. Perfume was just as much of a luxury item as it is now, stored in delicate ceramic bottles.

FACT

One of the Egyptians' most surprising inventions was the wig. The majority of Egyptian men shaved their heads. However, on special occasions, rich and powerful people such as priests would show their importance by wearing wigs made from human hair. The wig also protected its wearer from the heat of the sun.

LEISURE TIME

How do you like to spend your free time? Do you enjoy listening to music or getting together with friends for games? Some of the ways we spend our spare time are very new, but playing games, music, and sports are thousands of years old. The ancient Egyptians knew how to enjoy themselves. Many of the ways they chose to relax have remained popular ever since, from playing board games to keeping pets.

In the modern world, people generally have much more time to relax than they did in the past. Although our lives can seem incredibly busy, many of the everyday chores are done for us by washing machines and other devices. We buy food that is ready to eat from restaurants and supermarkets. In ancient Egypt, only the wealthier families could expect to have much spare time, as they had servants to do the daily chores for them.

MUSIC MAKERS

Music is something that people everywhere share. The music we make and listen to today has been influenced by people and cultures from many different times and places. No one can be sure what ancient Egyptian music sounded like. But we know that the musical instruments they used were the forerunners of many of the instruments we are now familiar with. Harps are still used in classical music today. The stringed lutes and lyres the Egyptians played eventually led to the guitars and violins of modern music. Ancient Egypt was also home to early brass and wind instruments, as well as drums and cymbals.

PLAYING GAMES

Gaming for you could mean playing the latest high-tech video gaming consoles with state-of-the-art graphics and superhero characters. The ancient Egyptians didn't have that choice, but they liked nothing more than developing their skills and strategies with board games.

The most popular board game was called Senet. Several Senet boards have been discovered in tombs of wealthy Egyptians. It was probably similar to the modern game of backgammon. Unfortunately, no rules have been found so we can't be sure how the game was played.

In the tomb of Nefertari, queen of Ramses II, Nefertari is painted playing Senet.

Hounds and jackals was another popular game, in which playing pieces with the heads of dogs and jackals raced each other around a board.

TOYS FOR THE CHILDREN

You may think that toys have changed completely since the time of the ancient Egyptians. Of course, today's toys look very different. They are made of materials such as plastic that were unknown to the Egyptians, and they use the latest technology. But the types of toys we grew up with didn't change all that much from ancient times.

The Egyptians played with dolls and model figures just as children do today, although theirs were not based on blockbuster movies. Egyptian children played with clay dolls and rag dolls made from linen. Children also played outdoors. Wood and leather balls show that ball games were popular. However, they had much less time for play than kids do now. Children were expected to help with chores or work in the fields at a young age.

Hunting and fishing are also pastimes that we share with the ancient Egyptians. For the ordinary people, these

FACT

Egyptians seemed to value physical fitness. The Heb-Sed festival of ancient Egypt celebrated the unity of Upper and Lower Egypt. It required the pharaoh to run a track four times in the festival's ritual. To do so, the pharaoh had to exercise to prepare. However, some wealthy Egyptians such as priests and scribes were depicted as being overweight.

provided a valuable source of food. For the upper class, they were also sport.

KEEPING PETS

Do you have any pets in your family? Dogs and cats are still the most popular choices. But many of us also like to keep more exotic animals such as snakes or lizards. You may be surprised to know that the ancient Egyptians were among the first people to keep pets. One tomb painting shows a boy walking a dog on a leash. In addition to dogs and cats, ancient Egypt had its share of more unusual pets, including monkeys, fish, and even hippos. One priestess was buried along with her pet monkey.

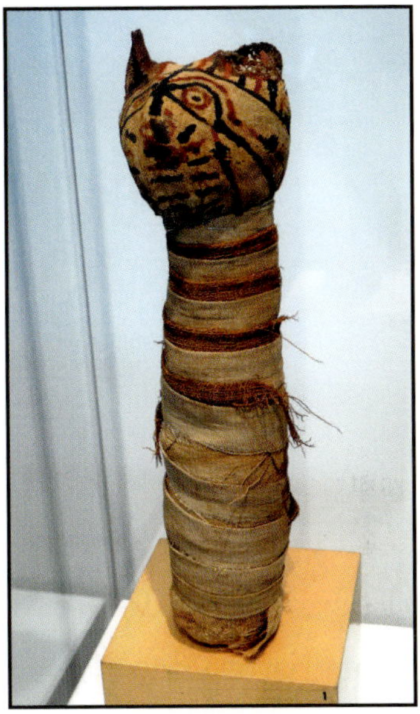

Many mummified cats have been found from ancient Egypt. Over time, cats came to be seen as sacred animals. The goddess Bastet was pictured as a woman with a cat's head.

Most of all, the Egyptians loved cats. This started because cats were good at catching the rats and mice that ate their crops, but many cats became pampered pets. Mummified cats were often buried with their owners. Some were even given their own tombs and contained gifts they would need in the afterlife.

CHAPTER 6

MEDICINE AND MUMMIES

If you've ever broken a bone, you know how important doctors are for fixing you up again! We all hope that we don't have to visit the doctor too often. When we do, we are grateful for all the knowledge that doctors and nurses have gained through years of training. Much of their knowledge is based on the latest research and discoveries, but they are also building on the work of doctors over thousands of years. From the first giant steps in understanding how the human body works, we must thank the medical discoveries of ancient Egypt.

Egyptian doctors were respected throughout the ancient world for their knowledge of the human body and treating diseases. Other civilizations such as the ancient Greeks and Romans built on what they learned from ancient Egypt. This became the basis of modern medicine.

Egyptians even performed operations on people's eyes. A papyrus shows an eye doctor treating a patient.

Some of the Egyptians' discoveries were lost for centuries and then rediscovered. Their understanding that blood circulated from the heart to the other organs of the body is one of these examples.

Ancient Egyptian doctors were good at treating injuries. Broken bones were set using wood bound with linen bandages to straighten the bone. The kit used by surgeons included sharp knives and forceps, similar to but much more basic than the tools used by modern surgeons.

Today's doctors have many years of training, medical books, and technology to help them treat different illnesses. Ancient Egyptian doctors, who were usually also priests, could consult medical papyruses. Papyruses would often guide doctors on a particular form of illness. One unearthed document deals with eye and skin problems. These documents were translated into Greek and other languages in the later years of Egyptian civilization.

FACT

Egyptian doctors did not understand everything. They believed that the heart controlled the body and the brain was less important. We now know that our bodies would not work at all without the brain.

A VISIT TO THE DOCTOR

Remember what happened at your most recent visit to the doctor when you were sick or hurt. The doctor asked you about your condition and then probably examined you. A visit to see the doctor in ancient Egypt followed the same pattern as it does today. After the examination, the doctor would decide if the patient could be treated. The doctor would even recommend a medicine if needed, including how much and when it should be taken. While those things sound familiar, Egyptian physicians often included a prayer or a chant as part of the cure, unlike modern medicine.

Egyptian physicians often included a prayer or a chant as part of the cure, unlike modern medicine.

Remedies often included things that are still thought to be beneficial. Patients were told to put raw meat on a cut before stitching it up. Meat contains a substance that helps cuts to heal. Other medicines included natural antiseptics such as honey and cinnamon, which are known to kill some germs.

FACT

Egyptian doctors could be male or female. The first female doctor that we know of was named Merit-Ptah. She lived around 2700 BC. It would be thousands of years before female doctors were common in other societies.

LEARNING FROM MUMMIES

A lot of what the Egyptians learned about medicine came from their beliefs about what happened after they died. They believed that dead people would need their bodies in the next life, so they mummified, or preserved, them. This process also helps us understand more about the lives of ancient Egyptians.

Mummification was usually reserved for the wealthy in Egyptian society. It involved removing the brain and other organs of a body, apart from the heart. The body was then dried over several weeks using a substance called natron. Mummy preparers wrapped the body in up to 30 layers of linen bandages to stop air from reaching it. The whole process took around 10 weeks, but the bodies remained well preserved for thousands of years until they were examined by modern archaeologists.

UNWRAPPING THE MUMMIES' SECRETS

Scientists use the latest technology to discover more about the life and death of ancient Egyptians. X-rays and scanners can be used to study their mummified bodies without unwrapping them. Taking tiny samples of body tissue can also reveal all sorts of information about the ways people lived, including what they ate. The study of mummies can also teach scientists about the diseases people suffered from in the past. In turn, this study can help to understand and treat illnesses in the modern world.

Modern scientists study a mummy from a scan. Their findings teach them about ancient and modern times.

FAMILIAR BUT DIFFERENT

Some parts of Ancient Egyptian society seem so familiar, from the food people ate to the toys children played with. We can forget that the artifacts that give us much of our knowledge are more than 2,000 years old. When we focus on the aspects of ancient Egypt that make sense to us, it's easy to forget that there were also many elements that were very different.

As one of the first great civilizations, the ancient Egyptians had to invent or discover almost everything they needed in their world. They learned how to grow enough food to feed everyone and to pay those who built the temples and monuments that survive along the Nile River. They discovered how to govern themselves effectively, how to communicate in writing, and much more that has been essential to most societies ever since.

The Egyptians collected crops as taxes and people could exchange the crops and goods they produced for other things they needed. Therefore they had no need for money until later in their civilization. They traveled along the river, so they had no need to invent wheeled vehicles. The pharaohs imported chariots from other civilizations later on, but these were used by the army for speed rather than for transporting goods or common people.

Ancient Egyptian civilization did not end suddenly. Its power and influence gradually faded over several centuries until it was taken over by other civilizations

The tomb of Ramses IV in the Valley of Kings is one of many examples containing rich art depicting life in ancient Egypt.

that wanted to build their own empires. From around 700 BC, Egypt's rulers battled against invaders from the Assyrian Empire in the East and then the Persians. In 332 BC, Egypt came under the control of Alexander the Great. In another 300 years, Egypt became part of the Roman Empire after the death of its last queen, Cleopatra.

The Greeks and Romans learned much from ancient Egypt, such as their skills in building and science. But many of Egypt's great innovations were lost and had to be rediscovered. Archaeologists have been able to piece together the details of Egyptian civilization by exploring tombs and decoding their writing to reveal the influence of ancient Egypt on later societies right up to the present day.

Even a model of a porch and garden was made to be placed in a tomb for its benefits in the afterlife. The model shows how spouts were used to catch the small amounts of rain that would fall.

INSIDE AN EGYPTIAN TOMB

Egyptian beliefs about the afterlife seem very strange to us, but without those beliefs our understanding of these amazing people would be much poorer. Egyptians were buried with everything they would need in the afterlife. For wealthy people, and especially the pharaohs, this meant they were buried with clothes, chariots, and much more, including models of everyday life, such as people plowing the fields and baking bread. These things show us all about life in ancient Egypt. Using this information, archaeologists can piece together the secrets of this amazing society.

A detailed model granary from about 1975 BC shows a full scene of Egyptian daily life. Figures of men were made to carry sacks of grain while the others include scribes tracking measurements.

GLOSSARY

antiseptic—prevents the growth of germs that can cause disease

archaeologist—someone who studies the remains and objects left behind by ancient people to learn more about their lives and society

democratic—describes government that is chosen in an election by the people it governs

fertile—describes ground that is suitable for growing crops

geometry—branch of math related to shapes and angles

glassblowing—process of making glass objects by blowing air into molten glass

granary—storehouse for grain and other food

hieratic—simplified form of ancient Egyptian writing used for everyday documents

hieroglyphic—form of Egyptian writing using images and symbols

inscription—words or images carved into stone or other hard material

irrigate—the use of canals or other methods to carry water from a river to water crops in fields

kohl—eye makeup made by grinding up dark-colored minerals

mummify—to preserve a body as a mummy

nome—administrative district of ancient Egypt

obelisk—four-sided pillar on a square base with a pyramid-shaped top, which typically stood at the entrance to Egyptian temples

papyrus—a reed plant that the ancient Egyptians used for many functions, including making paper; the plural form is *papyri*

scribe—person who was trained to read and write hieroglyphs and who often worked as a priest or government official

social security—a system to provide food or financial help to people in need

symbol—image designed to represent something else, such as a sound, word, or idea

tomb—place where a dead person is buried, which in ancient Egypt could be very elaborate for royalty or wealthy people

ADDITIONAL RESOURCES

Read More

Adamson, Heather. *Ancient Egypt: An Interactive History Adventure*. North Mankato, MN: Capstone, 2016.

Bow, James. *Forensic Investigations of the Ancient Egyptians*. New York: Crabtree Publishing, 2018.

Machajewski, Sarah. *A Kid's Life in Ancient Egypt*. New York: PowerKids Press, 2015.

Morley, Jacqueline and David Antram. *You Wouldn't Want to Be a Pyramid Builder!: A Hazardous Job You'd Rather Not Have*. New York: Franklin Watts, 2014.

Internet Sites

DK Find Out!: Ancient Egypt
https://www.dkfindout.com/uk/history/ancient-egypt/

Smithsonian: Ancient Egypt
https://www.si.edu/spotlight/ancient-egypt

National Geographic: Ancient Egypt 101
https://www.youtube.com/watch?v=hO1tzmi1V5g

BBC: 360° Travel inside the Great Pyramid of Giza
https://www.youtube.com/watch?v=TMzouTzim0o

SELECT BIBLIOGRAPHY

Aldred, Cyril. *The Egyptians*. 3rd ed. London: Thames & Hudson, 1998.

"Ancient Egypt." *The British Museum*. https://www.britishmuseum.org/learning/schools_and_teachers/resources/cultures/ancient_egypt.aspx Accessed August 4, 2019.

"Ancient Egypt." *The British Museum Online*. http://www.ancientegypt.co.uk/ Accessed August 4, 2019.

Ancient History Encyclopedia. https://www.ancient.eu Accessed August 4, 2019.

Booth, Charlotte. *An Illustrated Introduction to Ancient Egypt*. Stroud, UK: Amberley Publishing, 2014.

Dorman, Peter F., Alan K. Bowman, et al., "Ancient Egypt." *Encyclopaedia Britannica*. February 28, 2019. https://www.britannica.com/place/ancient-Egypt Accessed August 4, 2019.

"Egyptian Chronology." *University College London: Digital Egypt for Universities*. https://www.ucl.ac.uk/museums-static/digitalegypt/chronology/index.html Accessed August 4, 2019.

"Egyptian Mathematics." *The Story of Mathematics*. https://www.storyofmathematics.com/egyptian.html Accessed August 4, 2019.

Gill, Anton. *Ancient Egyptians: The Kingdom of the Pharaohs Brought to Life*. London: HarperCollins, 2003.

MacGregor, Neil. *A History of the World in 100 Objects*. London: Allen Lane, 2010.

Moorhouse, Dan. "Ancient Egyptian Medicine." *Medicine Through Time*. http://medicinethroughtime.co.uk/history/history-of-medicine/ancient-egyptian/#.XNvzIy3Mxok Accessed August 4, 2019.

National Geographic. "The World's Oldest Dress." *National Geographic*. https://www.nationalgeographic.co.uk/history-and-civilisation/2017/11/worlds-oldest-dress Accessed August 4, 2019.

Regulski, Ilona. "The Origins and Early Development of Writing in Egypt." Oxford: Oxford University Press, 2016. https://www.oxfordhandbooks.com/view/10.1093oxfordhb/9780199935413.001.0001/oxfordhb-9780199935413-e-61 Accessed August 4, 2019.

Tyldesley, Joyce. "Egypt and the Modern World" *BBC: Egyptians*. http://www.bbc.co.uk/history/ancient/egyptians/egypt_importance_01.shtml Accessed August 4, 2019.

About the Author

Nick Hunter has written more than 100 books for young people. He has a degree in modern history and specializes in writing about history and social studies. Before becoming an author, Nick worked in children's publishing for many years. He lives in Oxford, UK, with his wife and two sons.

INDEX